Beverly's Garden

Beverly's GARDEN

By

Gary Crone

Photo Contributors:

Philip T. Crone, Jeffrey Crone, Larry Crone, Beverly Crone

With Assistance From:

Lindsey Crone, Terry Crone, Michele Watson Crone

1st Edition

Leesburg, Virginia

BEVERLY'S GARDEN by Gary Crone

© 2014 by Gary Crone. All rights reserved.

No part of this book may be reproduced in any form or by any electronic or mechanical means including information storage and retrieval systems without permission in writing from the author.

For more information about this book, please write to the following address:
Beverly's Garden
PO Box 1419
Leesburg, VA 20177

Book design: Gary Crone
Cover photo: Larry Crone
ISBN 978-0-9907367-9-0

1st Edition

Printed in United States by Ingram

For Grandma, who loves her garden and all who sit with her there.

The Garden

In early May a warming light cheerfully shines in sweet delight—
Letting her know the time's at hand for joining with her earthen band.

*Returning to a barren ground where flowery friends will soon abound—
She'll bow her head and bend a knee as gardeners do to set plants free.*

Drawn down to feel the soil in hand, laboring long before she'll stand—

Lingering there until she's learned, how each friend fared and who returned.

Tending and weeding most the day, to guide their growth along the way— she lets her worries drift astray, in pure delight and endless play.

And as her friends begin to grow, they leaf and bloom as if to know—
They're in good hands with one so fair who tends them with loving care.

*Thru pickling sun or falling rains, she lingers long in lazy lanes—
Protecting paths of shaded scent, so all who enter may leave content.*

*And as the summer season unfolds, the garden is soon a sight to behold—
Rainbows of pedals now fill the day and tickled butterflies dance and sway.*

Until one day the morning guise, begins to signal their demise—
Bringing a fall that soon will cast, a darkened dot on plants failing fast.

Still in the dimming light each day, she toils to keep the cold at bay—

Standing watch thru fall's bitter end guarding her friends round winter's bend.

Working on, 'till the last pedals fold, from chilling winds—relentless cold.
And when at last the time has come, and nothing's left but winter's numb—

She gently lays them all to rest, knowing each friend has done their best—

In beds of earth where each will stay— already planning for next May.

Some Friends

Spring Daffodils

Purple Coneflowers

Mock Orange Hydrangea

Yellow Easter Lilly

Somewhere over the rainbow…

Multiflora Petunias

Pink Yarrow Varieties

Yellow Daylily

Ducks and her chicks

Red Lilies

Fancy Leaved Caladium

A Black Swallowtail Visits

Vibrant Orange Begonia

Yellow Coneflower Daisy

Miniature Red Moose Petunia

Grandiflora Petunias

Ruffle Edged Lemon Daylily

Ajuga (Bugleweeds)

Lily of the Valley

Shasta Daisies

Visit from a Monarch

Purple Spirea

Crème Brule Coreopsis

"Husker Red" Penstemon

Rose Campion

Purple Peony

Sterntaler Coreopsis (Tickweed)

Star of Bethlehem

Imperial Butterfly Bush

Antigua Marigolds

Lavender Hostas

"Already planning for next May"

CPSIA information can be obtained at www.ICGtesting.com
Printed in the USA
BVIW12n1724201217
503328BV00003B/3